Japanese Book Illustration

YU-YING BROWN

The British Library

Published by
The British Library,
Great Russell Street
London WC1B 3DG

and 27 South Main Street,
Wolfboro, New Hampshire
03894-2069

British Library Cataloguing in Publication Data

Brown, Yu-Ying
   Japanese book illustration.
   1. Japanese illustrations. Illustrations for books,
   1600-1900
   I. Title   II. British Library
   741.64'0952

   ISBN 0-7123-0128-3

Designed by Roger Davies
Typeset in Monophoto Ehrhardt by August
Filmsetting, Haydock, St Helens
Origination by York House Graphics,
Hanwell
Printed in England by Jolly and Barber Ltd,
Rugby

ACKNOWLEDGEMENTS
The author and publishers are grateful to the
Trustees of the British Museum for
permission to reproduce illustrations in this
book; **69**, **70**, and that on the inside cover.

NOTE
Names are written in accordance with
Japanese custom i.e. surname followed by
personal or art/studio name. However, artists
who died before 1900 are often referred to by
the latter alone. For consistency, the
prevailing modified Hepburn system of
transliteration has been used for all names
and titles, leaving consonant 'n' unchanged
to 'm' before b, m, p. Thus it is now Bunpō,
not Bumpō.

FRONT COVER
Courtesan reading a picture-book (detail).
One of 167 girls depicted in *Ehon seirō bijin
awase*, 'Picture-book Comparing the Beauties
of the Green Houses', by Suzuki Harunobu.
Five volumes, colour-printed with gauffrage
(1770, Edo). A monumental book that star-
ted the age of full-colour printing in Japan.
(*See also* page 23.)
[Or.75.g.34]

TITLE PAGE
Three varieties of *Nanten (Nandina
domestica)* grown in antique pots, by Untei.
From *Sōmoku kihin kagami*, 'Mirror of Rare
Plants and Trees', compiled and published
by Kinta, a gardener of Aoyama. Various
artists; three volumes, hand-coloured (Edo,
1827). [16033.c.3]

CONTENTS PAGE
Girl reading under a *kotatsu* (foot warmer)
using her arms as a pillow. From *Yamato
jinbutsu gafu* 'Picture-album of the Natives of
Yamato'. (*See also* **26**.)
[16112.b1]

BACK COVER
Warrior Asahina reclining under a *kotatsu*
along with his sword, comics, poetry slips
and pot plant. From the de luxe *kyōka* book,
Momo saezuri, 'A Hundred Twitterings',
contributed by Shunman, Tōrin (illustrated),
Shōhō and Unpō. *Orihon* album, colour-
printed (Edo, 1796).
[16099.c.83]

IINSIDE COVERS
A wood-block for an illustration in *Nihon
meisan zue*, reproduced from a Meiji recut.
(*See also* **35**.)

Contents

1

Utamaro, one of the world's greatest draftsmen decorating the interior of a 'Green House' with a painting of a giant phoenix, watched by admiring courtesans. From his *Seirō ehon nenjū gyōji* (*see also* **61**).

Introduction

Today Japan produces more high-quality illustrated publications than perhaps any other nation. This national penchant for pictures owes something to the calligraphy of her written word: a fluid combination of Chinese characters and flowing *hiragana* script – a combination in itself a form of pictorial expression. Indeed, the language of the brush seems as natural to the Japanese as speech. This native inclination, informed by technical skills imported from China, has resulted in a tradition of book illustration which dates back to the painted narrative handscrolls (*emakimono*) of the 8th century.

However, it was with the wood-block prints, contained in book or album, of the Edo period (1600–1868), that Japan came into her own. Before that, the magnificent *emakimono* were for the aristocratic few, while during the 800 years of Buddhist monopoly of printing, only a few books (mainly religious texts) were illustrated. Moreover, their woodcuts, though not without rustic charm, were in no way distinctive, being invariably copied from Chinese exemplars.

The cultural setting

The flowering of popular culture during the Edo period was to bring about a revolution in Japan's publishing practice and the art of the book. It was a period of unprecedented peace and stability, maintained for over 250 years by deliberate isolation from the outside world and by feudal control exercised within a rigidly stratified social system. The *samurai* were the rulers while the other groups – farmers, artisans and merchants, in descending order of status – constituted the ruled. However, the rapid expansion of the cities of Kyoto, Osaka, and – above all – the new capital of Edo (today's Tokyo) created a new townsmen (*chōnin*) culture that was to cut across class divides. The reading and artistic circles were no longer confined to the aristocracy and the *samurai*. With prosperity and the spread of literacy, especially among the hitherto despised merchants, there arose a great variety of popular reading material. Devotees of this or that art or discipline also began to emerge within the

2
Hokusai's caricature of a virtuoso artist in Chinese garb inscribing the title of his book with all four 'paws', while a boy apprentice looks up in admiration. Frontispiece to *Ehon saishiki-tsū*, 'Mastering Painting in Colours', written and illustrated by Hokusai in his 89th year. Two volumes (Edo, 1848).
[16112.a.12]

leisured bourgeoisie. Printing houses proliferated to well over 1,500, and between them issued a huge corpus of publications on every conceivable subject, the majority of which were profusely illustrated with woodcuts. The coverage closely corresponds to commercial publishing in the West today, except that the list was graced by the work of many outstanding artists, representing a variety of styles and schools.

The significance of Japanese illustrated books and albums in the history of the world's graphic art has been comprehensively and excitingly appraised by Jack Hillier in his latest study *The Art of the Japanese Book*. The present book, however, seeks to focus on the illustrative, rather than the purely artistic, aspects. Accordingly, the examples are drawn almost entirely from the British Library's own extensive holdings. These have been built up over three centuries from the legacies of four inspired collectors: Engelbert Kaempfer (1651–1716), Philipp Franz Von Siebold (1796–1866), Ernest Satow (1843–1928) and William Anderson (1842–1900). Taken as a whole, they are stronger in *eirihon* ('books with pictures inserted') than in *ehon* (picture-books) or *gafu* (drawing-books), the two genres in which the artists' works took precedence over any text. Some of the masterpieces of *ehon* and *gafu* were transferred over the years before 1973, when the British Library was founded, to the Department of Oriental Antiquities (now Japanese Antiquities) of the British Museum, and are given more exposure in exhibitions and research. It is hoped that through the less familiar pieces here included, the reader may savour afresh some of the variety, virtuosity and sheer delight of Japanese book illustration.

The topics under which specific works or pictures are grouped are not to be taken as bases for bibliographical exactitude, but just as a means to present, in relation to literary and social trends, a limited selection from an enormous field. A few manuscript items are included (**3–6; 27; 28; 31; 32**) to show the transition from painted to printed works, and to provide a broader perspective.

Schools and techniques

Whereas in China book illustration was deemed beneath any self-respecting artist, in Japan it became a creative medium for painters of the major schools: the Tosa, Kanō, *Ukiyo-e*, *Nanga* and Maruyama-Shijō. The establishment schools of Tosa and Kanō were named after their respective founders, Tosa Mitsunobu (1434–1525) and Kanō Masanobu (1434–1530). They maintained the academic style of the previous centuries and provided basic training to many artists from other schools. The former was patronised by the court nobles and sought to preserve the native style of painting, the *Yamato-e* ('Japanese pictures'). The latter, favoured by the military government, was closely associated with Zen and Chinese *suiboku-ga* (black ink painting). *Ukiyo-e* (pictures of the 'floating world'), the best known of all schools, concerned itself primarily with depicting the world of pleasure and entertainment which flourished in the great cities. *Nanga* ('southern painting') was inspired by the intuitive, amateurish painting style of the Chinese scholar, or literati (*bunjin*). The compound, Maruyama-Shijō, on the other hand, was derived from the name of the founder Maruyama Ōkyo (1733–95) and Shijō street in Kyoto on which the studio of his associate Matsumura Goshun (1752–1811) stood. Though Goshun founded his own school, both he and Ōkyo proclaimed Nature as their direct teacher, preferring to sketch from life rather than copy old masters as often practised by the Tosa and Kanō. Hence, the two schools are together referred to as the naturalistic school, the shorter name Shijō being used for both. Also, since the *Nanga*, and Maruyama-Shijō were each based in the old capital of Kyoto and since both sought to capture the inner spirit of whatever was depicted, they are sometimes collectively known as the classical or impressionistic school, in contrast with the representational *Ukiyo-e* in vogue in the upstart city of Edo.

The making of the traditional Japanese book differed fundamentally from that of the West in that everything was hand-crafted as opposed to machine-made. Such books were tasteful and unpretentious in a way almost unique to Japanese culture. The three principal forms of binding that need concern us here were *makimono* ('rolled object' or handscroll); *orihon* (folding or concertina book); and *fukurotoji* (thread-sewn 'bag binding'), all of which had originated in China. Of these, the last named was perhaps the least known in the West. It was, however, the most widely used in the Far East. The earlier handscroll had the disadvantage of being unwieldy, while the *orihon* needed heavier quality paper which was expensive and wore out printing blocks faster. With *fukurotoji* (which consists of a series of sheets with printing on one surface only, each folded down the centre to form a double leaf stitched at the loose ends) one could use the usual thin, supple, and often transluscent handmade paper without backing and yet the design or text showed through very little. However, this style of binding necessitated the facing pages of an open book, the recto on the right-hand sheet and the

verso on the left, being printed from two separate blocks. When an illustration is restricted to one side of the space, as is often the case in a Chinese book, no problem arises. But when it comes to a double-page spread, the Western reader may find the central gap or *nodo* puzzling. The Japanese artists used various ingenious devices to draw the viewer's eye from one page to the next, while making the central break an integral part of the design.

The printing process involved team-work between publisher, artist, block-cutter and printer. First the publisher, who usually owned the workshop where the finished products were also sold, commissioned a design from an artist (or a calligrapher in the case of text). The design, or a copy of it, was then pasted face down on a smooth block of wood (generally cherry). It was then cut to leave the design in sharp relief. Ink was applied to the raised design, and the sized paper laid on top. An impression was then taken by rubbing the upper or reverse side of the paper with a pad (called the *baren*). A striking feature of Japanese black-and-white prints (*sumizuri*) was the use of gradation techniques to produce a tonal effect of *sumi* ink akin to free, painterly brushwork.

However, it was in colour printing (using multiple blocks, one for each colour) that the Japanese excelled. Here, too, the technique originally derived from China where it had been known since the 16th century. The importation in 1720 through the port of Nagasaki, of the two famous coloured printed manuals of painting, the *Ten Bamboo Studio* and the *Mustard Seed Garden* made a lasting impact. The first Japanese attempts in the 1730s to use Chinese methods of colour registration met with but moderate success (15). Forty years later, however, the Japanese developed a simpler device known as the *kentō* to ensure more exact register. With it multi-colour wood-block printing was perfected and made economically profitable. There were isolated examples earlier, but it was the *Ukiyo-e* artist, Suzuki Harunobu (1724–70) who first exploited this new medium. In 1770, he effectively ushered in the age of 'brocade prints', so called because of the richness of their coloured patterns, with his much eulogised *Ehon seirō bijin awase* which depicts prettily clothed girls engaged in a round of elegant pastimes (*see* front cover).

Romances and folk-tales

Before the appearance in Kyoto in 1608 of the celebrated illustrated Saga edition of the *Ise monogatari*, the 'Tale of Ise' (8), literature of Japanese origin, including classical novels, legends and short stories, had existed only in manuscript format. Manuscripts with narrative paintings known as *Nara-ehon* (Nara picture-books), which flourished between the 16th and early 18th centuries, play an especially important part in disseminating medieval popular stories before they became widely available through commercial printing. With alternation of calligraphic text and graphic pictures, they recount such folk themes as the suffering of stepchildren; the humble diver's love for her high-ranking husband (4); marriages between humans and animals; the exploits of warriors, such as the legendary Benkei (6); and the quelling of monsters, demons and foreign invaders (3). Whether professionally

3

Yuriwaka (a Japanese corruption of Ulysses) leading
his army to repel the Mongol invasion. From *Yuriwaka
daijin*, 'The Grand Minister Yuriwaka'. *Nara-ehon*
painted manuscript. Three rolls, about 1650. This
unusual piece in the repertoire of the *kōwakamai*, chant-
and-dance stage art of the medieval period, was an
obvious adaptation of the Homeric epics. It was first
performed in 1551, two years after the arrival of the first
Jesuit in Japan.
[Or.13822]

meticulous or naively charming in their execution, carried out anonymously by either monks or artisan painters, *Nara-ehon* are colourful and often embellished with gold leaf. They were so popular that some of the 17th-century printed editions were hand-coloured by their publishers to simulate the *Nara-e* effect. These *tanroku-bon*, so called because of the predominance of orange (*tan*) and green (*roku*) in the tinting of the woodcut illustrations, are now highly prized on account of their rarity. The 'Tale of the Saga Brothers' (7) is one of the very few genuine *tanroku-bon* preserved in the West.

Nara-ehon were, in effect, the low-brow successors to the medieval narrative handscrolls by Tosa artists. The latter had been modelled on the great *Yamato-emaki* (handscrolls in the indigenous *Yamato-e* style) which flourished in the Heian (794–1185) and Kamakura (1185–1333) periods. Though with less finish and more akin to folk art, the *Nara-e* modifications retained many *Yamato-e*/Tosa characteristics: open roof projection, abbreviated facial features, and schematised cloud formations and pines (5). This style was to be adopted in the wood-block medium in black-and-white line drawings in all illustrated books before the advent of *Ukiyo-e*, *c*.1660 (9). These included the *Saga-bon Ise mongatari* mentioned above, and all the *kana-zōshi* (booklets written chiefly in *kana* syllabic script), a new genre of fiction catering for the newly literate 'man in the street'.

The term *Saga-bon* ('Saga book') refers to a series of Japanese classics printed by Suminokura Soan (1571–1632), a wealthy merchant and art connoisseur, at his printing press in Saga village near Kyoto. With the collaboration of his friend and mentor, the artist-calligrapher Hon'ami Kōetsu (1558–1637), Soan sought to recapture the refined elegance of Heian court life. This he did with tinted quality paper and a graceful calligraphy expressed in movable type, a technique newly imported from Korea. The *Ise monogatari* was hugely influential. Not only was it an example of the high culture of the Kyoto bourgeoisie, it also contained the earliest known, non-Buddhist, printed illustrations in native works of literature (8).

However, it was not until the arrival of *ukiyo-zōshi* (the floating world booklet) in the 1680s that illustrators began to sign their works. This expression of pride and desire for public recognition was due largely to Hishikawa Moronobu (*c*.1618–94), whose flair for depicting scenes from daily life set the basic style of the *Ukiyo-e* school. However, it was his younger contemporary Yoshida Hanbei (*fl.c.*1660–92) who pioneered the illustrations for several racy novels written by Ihara Saikaku (1642–93), the acknowledged master of the genre. The first, and still among the best known of his novels is *Kōshoku ichidai otoko* (12), the 'Man Who Spent His Life in Love'. Titles such as this well exemplify the underlying theme of the *ukiyo-zōshi*: the hedonistic pur-

4
The woman diver in a boat waiting to enter the Palace of the Dragon King to retrieve a precious jewel for Fujiwara no Kamatari, the 7th-century founder of the powerful Fujiwara clan. From *Taishokkan*, the 'Great Embroidered Cap'. *Nara-ehon* painted manuscript. Artist unknown, Tosa school; two rolls, about 1590.
[Or.12690]

5
Prince Genji's love at first sight of Utsusemi who was playing *gō* against her more showy step-daughter. From *Genji monogatari kotaba*, 'Extracts from the Tale of Genji'. Folding album of paintings accompanied by calligraphic texts. Artist: attributed to Sumiyoshi Jokei, a branch head of the Tosa-school; mid-17th century.
[Or.1287]

6 (*Page 12*):
Young Yoshitsune testing his swordsmanship against the warrior monk Benkei of legendary strength at the Gojō bridge in Kyoto. From *Benkei monogatari*, the 'Tale of Benkei'. *Nara-ehon* painted manuscript. Anonymous, Tosa school; two volumes; about 1660.
[Or.12439]

7 (*Page 13*):
The Soga brothers praying before avenging their father's death. From *Soga monogatari* 'The Tale of the Soga Brothers'. *Tanroku-bon* edition, hand-coloured. Artist unknown, Tosa school; 10 volumes; 1646.
[16052.f.2]

8
The unnamed hero has been humiliated by an imperial command that he serves as a falconer, feeling he was too old and dignified for the task. One of the 49 illustrations from *Ise monogatari*, the 'Tale of Ise'. *Saga-bon* edition, text printed from movable-type on tinted coloured paper. Artist unknown, Tosa school; two volumes (Kyoto, 1608). [Or.64.c.36]

9
Genji's romantic encounter with Yūgao. From the first illustrated edition of the 'Tale of Genji'. Artist unknown, Tosa school. 60 volumes, 1650.
[16055.b.1]

suit of sensual and material pleasure by well-to-do merchants denied political power or social standing.

Ple.sure seeking and the irony of its ultimate emptiness were to dominate a diversity of popular fiction from the mid-18th century onwards. Among these *gesaku* ('jestful writing') were *kibyōshi* (literally, 'yellow backs'), *yomihon* ('books for reading') and *gōkan* (combined volumes). The *kibyōshi* had been preceded in turn by *akahon* ('red books'), *kurohon* ('black books'), and *aohon* ('grass-green books') **(10)**. This group of novelettes, named after their cover colours, was not unlike the comic strips of today. They catered primarily for children and semi-literate women, and became the means whereby many eminent *Ukiyo-e* artists launched their careers.

The *yomihon* books were more erudite and often immensely long,

10 *(Left)*:
Cover designs of early novelettes by *Ukiyo-e* artists.
(Top left): An *akahon: Kintoki osanadachi*, 'Exploits of
the Wonder Child Kintoki'. Artist unknown. Two
volumes (Edo, *c*.1750). Note that the lead-red cover
has oxidised with age [16104.b.13/4]. *(Top right)*: A
kurohon: Tokitsukaza iribune Soga, 'The Soga
Brothers. A Kabuki programme for the first showing
at the Nakamuraza. Artist unknown. Two volumes,
(Edo, *c*.1758) [16104.a.23/2]. *(Bottom left)*: An *aohon;
Kantoku byakko no sama*, 'Fortune of the White Fox',
by Joa. Artist unknown. Two volumes (Edo, 1754).
[16104.b.13/5]. *(Bottom right)*: An *aohon: (Shinpan)
shian-kaku onna Imagawa*, 'Admonition of Imagawa
for Women', illustrated by Torii Kiyotsune. Three
volumes (Edo, 1767) [16108.a.50/3].

11
Matching cover illustrations. From *Sono yukari hina no
omokage*, a *gōkan* adaptation of the 'Tale of Genji', by
Keisai Eisen, Tanesada and Senka. Illustrated by
Kunisada and Yoshitora. Twenty-three parts, colour-
printed (Edo, 1847–64).
[16107.e.33]

12 *(Top)*:
A revelry scene in a 'Green House'.
From *Kōshoku ehon taizen*, the
'Escapades of an Amorous Man in
Pictures', an abridged picture-book
version of Ihara Saikaku's *Kōshoku
ichidai otoka*. Attributed to
Hishikawa Moronobu (Edo, 1686)
Volume II (of four); an extremely
rare book, no complete copy
known.
[16116.d.15]

13
A street brawl in front of a brothel
(right); an adulterer visiting his
lover. From *Bikei makie no matsu*,
an *ukiyo-zōshi* on the life of
pleasure quarters at Ise, the mecca
of Shinto pilgrimage, written by
Shichūken. Artist unknown,
Ukiyo-e school. Five volumes (?Ise,
1708).
[Or.75.f.30]

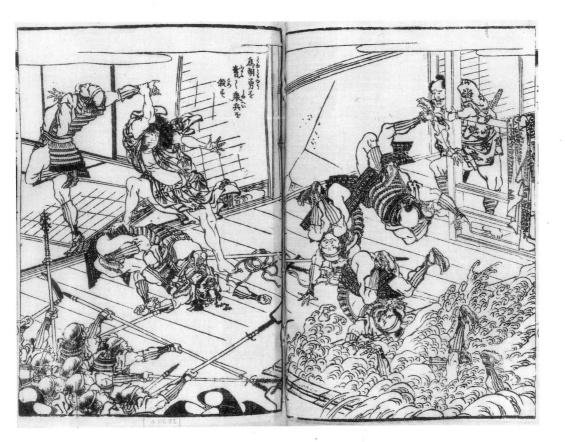

14
Tametomo, the Master
Archer, giving lethal blows to
his enemies. From *Chinsetsu
yumihari-zuki*, a *yomihon*
novel, based on the tragic
historical figure during the
Hōgen war. Written by Bakin
with illustrations by Hokusai.
Thirty volumes
(Edo,1807–11).
[16107.b.3]

some being serialised over several decades. Complex plots of heroism,
with miraculous twists and turns, were loosely based on remote historical events or borrowed from exotic foreign tales such as the Chinese
'Water Margin'. This genre was inspired by the combined genius of
Takizawa Bakin (1776–1848) and Katsushika Hokusai (1760–1849)
whose author–artist partnership produced many brilliantly illustrated
novels (**14**). Competition from the *yomihon* around 1800 led the
kibyōshi novelette to develop into the elaborate *gōkan*. Adaptations
from both Kabuki drama and *yomihon* were presented through
woodcuts and calligraphy, entirely filling every page. *Gōkan* were char-
acterised by bright, sometimes garish cover pictures printed from
multi-colour blocks (**11**). Their illustrations were very much the preserve of the Utagawa branch of the *Ukiyo-e*, with the famous Toyokuni
(1769–1825) as its head.

Poetry and poets

As popular culture flourished in the Edo period, poetry writing spread throughout society. Three variations of the classical 31-syllable *waka* (in stanzas of 5–7–5–7–7) evolved and attracted vast new audiences. *Haiku*, the 17-syllable verse linked to the seasons, was universally popular and is still much in vogue today. Originally the opening part of a *waka* sequence, it evolved independently when, with simple words and free thoughts, Matsuo Bashō (1644–94) made it accessible to commoners. The other two forms, developed for amusement, were *kyōka* (literally 'crazy verses') which parodied *waka* (**19**), and *senryū*, a satirical *haiku*, named after Karai Senryū (1718–90).

The genealogical development of these principal forms is evident from the fondness of the Japanese for iconographical portraits of their favourite poets and poetesses, ancient or modern. This tradition goes back to the 12th century, when *Yamato-e* painters depicted the 36 or 100 *waka* immortals, each with one of their best poems. It was Tosa artists who reproduced them in print, the earliest being the *Saga-bon* editions. Thus, imaginary portraits of poets seated on *tatami* dais became the model for many *waka* books (**16**) until, in the 17th century, Moronobu rendered them in the modish *Ukiyo-e* style. In his *Fūryū sugata-e hyakunin isshu* (**17**), stereotyped portrayals were replaced by poetry readers in contemporary dress, posturing facetiously.

Yosa Buson (1716–83), the great *haiku* revivalist and *Nanga* artist, left a book of portraits of his own disciples, drawn with minimal strokes, entitled *Haikai sanjū rokkasen*, 'Thirty-six Immortals of Haikai'. It was published posthumously in 1799 and inspired a succession of figure drawings in cursive style (**18**). In the *kyōka* sphere, portraitures enjoyed even greater vogue, engaging the talents of such *Ukiyo-e* masters as Kitagawa Utamaro (1754–1806), Kitao Masanobu (1761–1816) and Hokusai. *Michinoku-gami kyōka awase* (**24**), a book by Utagawa Toyohiro (1773–1828), is a fine and very rare example. Toyohiro, otherwise known for his landscapes, here depicted the thirteen pairs of *kyōka* poets with the graphic realism typical of *Ukiyo-e* figure studies.

Group motivation is a striking feature of Japanese poetry. Countless poetry circles, especially *haiku* and *kyōka*, were formed for competition and recreation. Thus, in *Kyōka Nihon fudoki* (**22**), we see men and women from all walks of life coming together for one such occasion. Often the societies arranged for their members' verses to be printed in anthologies. Of course, the brevity of Japanese poems made them ideally suited for pictorial representation. In fact, among the most beautiful of all Japanese illustrated books are poetry albums embellished by, more often than not, several artists (*see* The golden age).

Meanwhile, *haiku* books figured prominently in the advance of colour printing. The monumental *Chichi no on*, 'Love for a Father'

15
The 'Serenity of spring' – one of four colour-printed illustrations by Ogawa Ritsuō for the *Chichi no on*, a *haiku* anthology in memory of the actor Ichikawa Danjurō I. Two volumes; 1730, privately published. One of the earliest attempts at colour printing. This work also contains 66 *sumizuri* illustrations by Hanabusa Ippō.
[Or.74.cc.3]

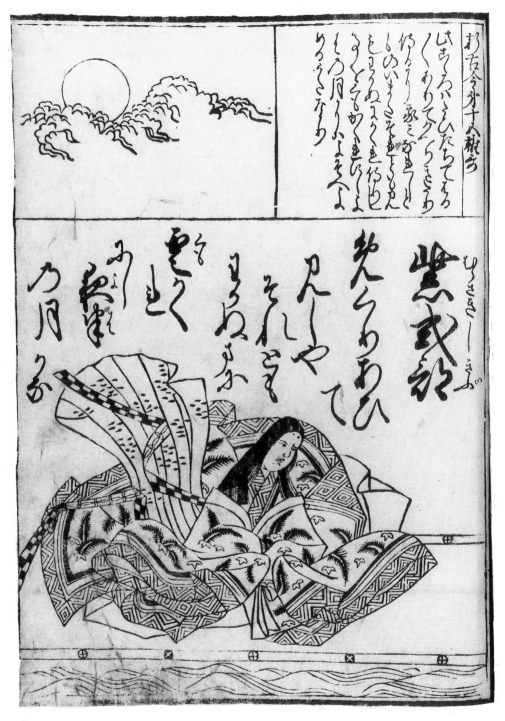

16

Lady Murasaki Shikibu, authoress of the 'Tale of Genji'. From *Kashiragaki eshō hyakunin isshu*, 'One Poem by Each of One Hundred Poets, Illustrated and with Head Notes'. Artist unknown, Tosa school (Kyoto, 1673). [Or.75.h.3]

17

Couple reading a poem by Okikaze on the theme of love: detail from *Fūryū sugatae hyakunin isshu*, the 'Fanciful Portraits of *Hyakunin Isshu*'. Attributed to Hishikawa Moronobu. Three volumes, partially hand-coloured (Edo, 1695).

[Or.65.a.12]

of 1730 (**15**), heralded polychrome printing in many such works. Among the finest early examples were the trilogy of Katsuma Ryūsui (1711–96), including *Umi no sachi*, the 'Boon of the Sea' of 1762 (**51**); and Harunobu's acclaimed *Ehon seirō bijin awase* of 1770. In the latter, each portrait is accompanied by a *haiku* poem composed by the courtesan depicted. *Chichi no on* was a *haiku* anthology compiled by Ichikawa Sansō in memory of his actor father, Ichikawa Danjurō I. Here the colour printing is decidely tentative; and the pretty roundel designs

18

A poet's messenger (detail), one of several cursive figure drawings with minimal strokes by Matsumura Goshun, founder of the Shijō school. From the *Shin hanatsumi*, 'New Flower Picking', the diary of Buson. One volume, lightly colour printed (Kyoto, *c.*1798). [16114.f.45]

19

Umbrellas over the faded cherry tree blossoms, a parody of Japanese feelings towards these best loved, transient flowers. From *Ryūkō meibutsu-shi*, 'Noted Products of the Willow Street'. *Kyōka* anthology with illustrations by Kabocha Sōen. One volume, lightly colour-printed (Edo, 1834). [16099.c.86]

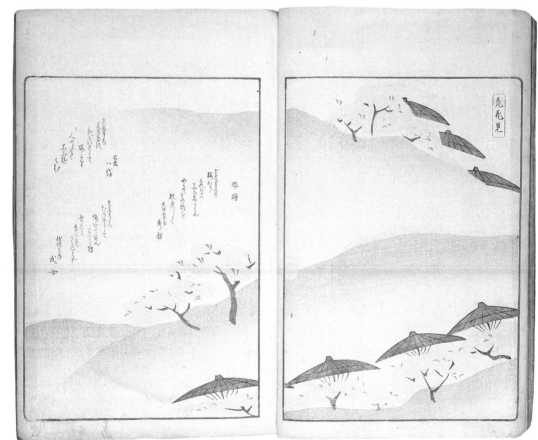

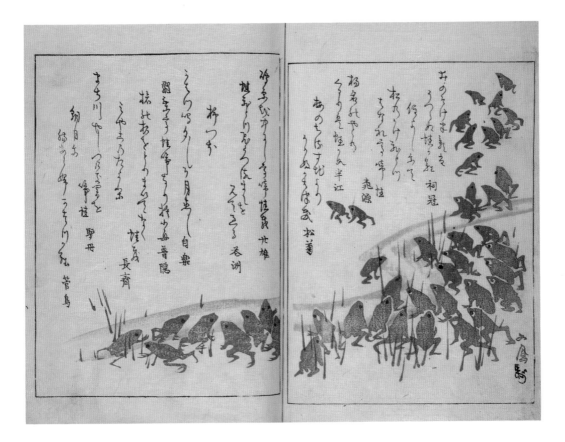

20
Frogs congregating by the stream, by Bunpō. From *Shin kawazu awase*, 'New Frogs' Matches', a *haiku* anthology on the theme of frogs. Various Shijō artists. One volume, lightly colour-printed (Kyoto, 1800). A witty image parodying Basho's famous *haiku*: 'An old pond: a frog jumps in – the sound of water'.
[Or.81.c.11]

betoken the indebtedness of the artist, Ogawa Ritsuō (1663–1747) to the Chinese painting manuals introduced to Japan about that time.

Chichi no on also set the style for the commemorative *haiku* publications of which *Shin hanatsumi*, 'New Flower Picking' (18) is perhaps most noteworthy. This book consists of poems and diary notes by Buson in his own distinct calligraphy, interspersed with a few figure drawings by his pupil, Matsumura Goshun. The latter is thought to have acquired the manuscript and then sought to preserve it in print in homage to his master. Sketchiness and brevity were the hallmarks of Shijō artists for whom *haiga* (pictures of *haiku*) were thus natural subjects. Chō Gesshō (1772–1832), Yamaguchi Soken (1759–1818) (26), and Kawamura Bunpō (1779–1821) were among the acknowledged masters whose free and rapid sketches are poetic in themselves. Bunpō's witty image of gregarious frogs (no doubt a pun on the single frog made famous in a *haiku* by Basho) (20), shows the virtue of sheer simplicity, perfect placing on the page, and harmony with the calligraphy. These are the supreme attributes of illustrated *haiku* books.

21
Girls dancing in the
moonlight at the *bon*
festival, by Ōishi Matora,
a Shijō artist. From
Shinji andon, 'Festival
Lanterns'. A *senryū*
anthology jointly
illustrated by Shijō and
Ukiyo-e artists. Five
volumes, colour-printed
(Nagoya, 1829–47).
[Or.65.a.29]

22 *(Page 28 top)*:
A gathering for *kyōka*
contest, with the artist
Gakutei (centre right)
presiding. From *Kyōka
Nihon fudoki*, a
'Topographical Record
of Japan with Kyōka'.
A *kyōka* anthology
illustrated by Yashima
Gakutei. One volume,
lightly colour-printed
(Osaka, 1831).
[16099.c.65]

23 *(Page 28 bottom)*:
A young man retiring
under a mosquito net
with a poem expressing
his loneliness. From
Shinobu-zuri,
'Recollection Prints', a
waka anthology,
illustrated by Kitao
Tokinobu (Sekkōsai), an
Ukiyo-e artist. Two
volumes, colour-printed
with stencil (Kyoto,
1750). This charming
little-known book is one
of the earliest examples
of stencil colour printing.
[Or.81.c.27]

今日
ぞこう里
姫の
ほうさ
盆踊

24 *(Page 29)*:
Portrait of a housewife *kyōka* poetess, with one of her comic poems in cursive calligraphy. From *Michinoku-gami kyōka awase*, 'Paper from Michinoku Provinces with *Kyōka* Verses' (provisional tltle). A *kyōka* anthology illustrated by Utagawa Toyohiro. One volume, colour-printed (Edo, 1793). The second extant copy so far located. [16099.c.90]

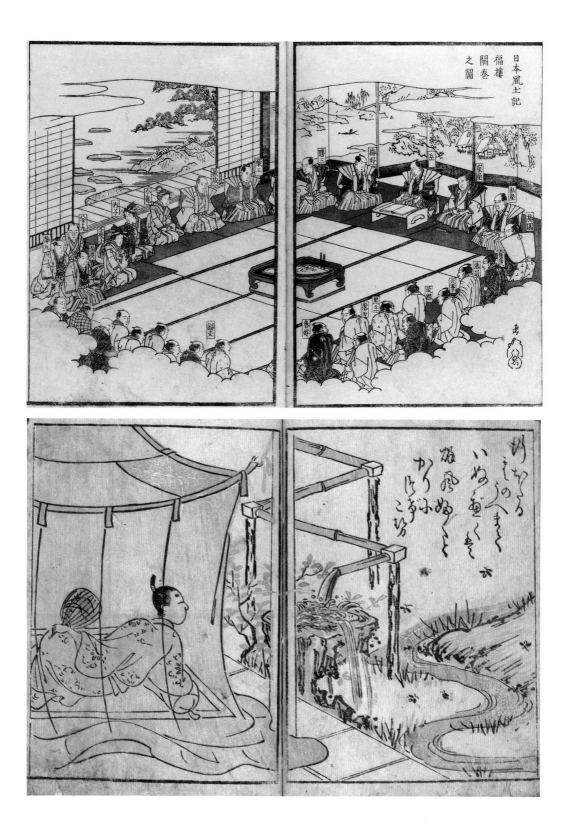

28

Guides and documentaries

The modern Japanese love of travel can be traced back to the Edo period, when, although going overseas was forbidden on pain of death, there was a craze for domestic tours. Initially, distance journeys had been limited almost entirely to *daimyō* progresses to Edo, for the attendances required periodically at the Shogun's court; group pilgrimages to temples and shrines; and the wanderings in quest of truth by such ascetic priests and poets as Bashō. However, once the sea and land routes between East and West Japan were opened up in 1672, ever larger numbers of townspeople took off on business or for recreation. They generated an upsurge of demand for route maps, printed **(25)** or manuscript **(28)**, as well as a new type of topographical literature known as *meisho-ki*, 'records of famous places'. These guidebooks not only provided them with essential information as regards distances and the availability of inns, but also detailed the history, lore, festivals, and products associated with each locality. From early on, many *Ukiyo-e* artists were involved in their profuse illustration. Among them were Hishikawa Moronobu who was to elevate mundane *meisho-ki* to veritable works of art **(29)**, and Ōmori Yoshikiyo (*fl*.1701–16) **(39)**. The genre reached its acme in the 1770s, covering not only big cities but also the most remote provinces. Meanwhile, directories of top courtesans and the pleasure quarters were produced in great number **(31)**, as were the itinerary maps picturing the 53 stations of the Tokaido **(30)**, the 351-mile coastal highway from Edo to Kyoto made world-famous by Hiroshige's broadsheet prints.

The immediate forerunners of the *meisho-ki* were the *fūzoku-ga*, a mode of painting depicting the activities and appearance of people in

26
Traveller on a donkey, with
driver. From *Yamato jinbutsu
gafu*, 'Picture-album of the
Natives of Yamato', one of the
most admired drawing books
by Yamaguchi Soken of the
Maruyama school. Three
volumes (Kyoto, 1800). (*See
also* contents page.)
[16112.b.1]

contemporary settings. It flourished from the 1570s to the end of the
17th century and was executed largely on folding screens by artists of
the Tosa or related Sumiyoshi school. The 50, recently discovered,
handscroll-sized paintings from the Kaempfer collection of the pre-
1693 vintage are fine examples of this genre (**27**). In them, the panor-
amas of shrines, temples and other scenic sites were considerably
enlivened by vignettes of people engaging in all sorts of occupations
and entertainments. They thus suggested a heightened awareness of
everybody's place in the secular world, an awareness that was to find
the fullest expression in the *Ukiyo-e* art of the next century.

Picturesque landscapes and leisured excursions were not the only
popular subjects for pictorial recording in guide and documentaries
(**36**). In fact, the Japanese had an inordinate interest in depicting their
own occupational classes, especially craftsmen, at work (**34**). Meanwhile, foreigners, including their closest neighbours, the Chinese and
Koreans, were objects of insatiable curiosity. During the seclusion
period, they were so rarely encountered that any visitation was guaran-
teed to cause a commotion (**37, 38, 39**).

Another category of illustrated guidebooks was the *meisan zue* (pictorial accounts of famous products) which give matter-of-fact records

27 (*Opposite above*):
Kaleidoscope of theatre and other entertainments by the Kamo river in Kyoto. Note the naked swimmers about to go into the river. They are probably urban outcasts who lived on things caught in the river with their bare hands.

(*Opposite below*):
Pilgrimage to a temple in Amanohashidate, one of the three famed sights of Japan. From a set of 50 handscroll-sized paintings brought back by Kaempfer in 1693. Artist unknown, Tosa–Sumiyoshi school. One album, probably remounted from a scroll; no date known, *c.* the Kanbun era (1661–72).
[Add.5252]

28
Nagasaki and the surrounding islets in southernmost Japan. Deshima, the tiny enclave for Dutch traders was shown in exaggerated proportion in the centre. From *Edo yori Nagasaki made (yado tsuki) funamichi meisho kyūseki* 'Sea Routes between Edo and Nagasaki with Famous Inns and Sites Indicated'. Painted manuscript maps, anonymous, two rolls, remounted in *orihon*, late 17th century. Ex-Siebold collection.
[Maps 12.c.25: roll A and Or.2875: roll B].

of the production of everyday necessities as well as consumer goods (**35**). Alongside them stand numerous painted manuscripts officially commissioned to 'photograph' agricultural and industrial silks, ranging from farming, fishing, mining (**32**), and metal-founding, to canal construction (**33**). All in all, these guides and documentaries are a mine of information on the social, economic and cultural history of Edo Japan.

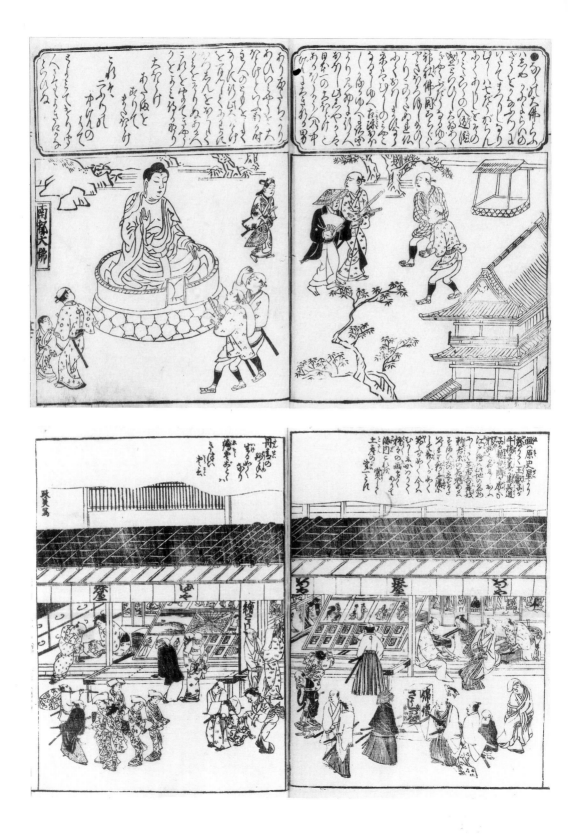

34

29 (*Opposite above*):
Pilgrimage to the Big Buddha
in Nara. From *Wakoku meisho
kagami*, 'A Mirror of Famous
Sites of Japan', by Hishikawa
Monorobu. Three volumes
(Edo, 1682). Note the text was
relegated to the upper third of
the page, giving more
prominence to the picture. An
early picture-book format
innovated by Monorobu.
[Or.75.g.36]

30 (*Opposite below*):
Travellers acquiring
picture books and prints,
the famous products of
Edo, as souvenirs from
wayside bookshops, by
Masayoshi. From *Tōkaidō
meisho zue*, 'Pictorial
Accounts of the Well-
known Places on the
Tōkaidō'. Compiled by
Akisato Ritō and illustrated
by various artists of mixed
schools. Six volumes
(Osaka, 1797).
[16114.a.8]

31
Modish clientele being
entertained by courtesans; a
customer is resting with too
much *sake*. From *Yoshiwara
koi no michibiki*, 'Guide to
the Way of Love in
Yoshiwara', illustrated by
Hishikawa Moronobu. One
volume, partly hand-
coloured (Edo, 1678).
[16107.a.35]

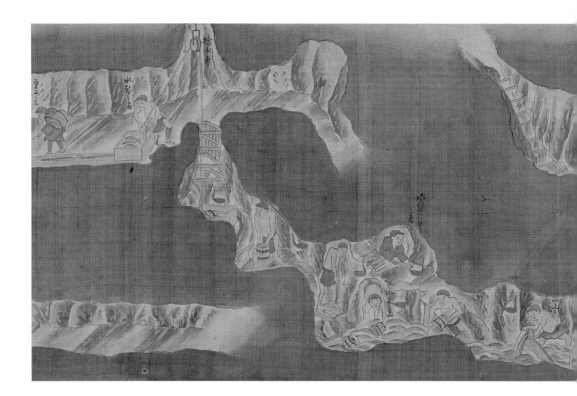

32
Gold miners at work in
tunnels. From a set of three
scrolls after the *Sado kōzan
sho-kasegikata emaki*
(1716–36), 'Picture-scroll
Depicting the Various Stages
of Mining in Sado'.
Anonymous; three rolls, ink
and colour on silk; about 1800.
Ex-Siebold collection. Sado
Island was declared special
territory under direct control
of the Shogunate when gold
was discovered around 1600.
[Or.918–20]

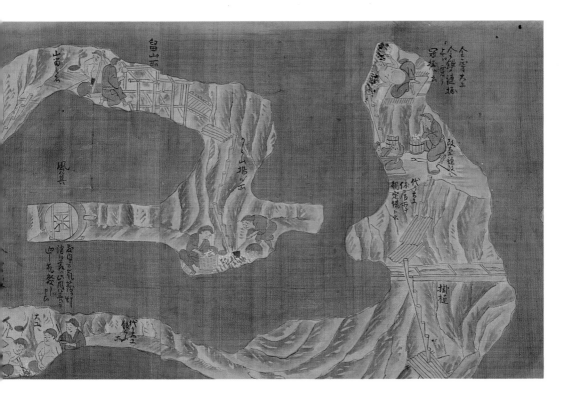

33
Villagers digging the canal
under official supervision in
the marshy district of Inban.
From *Shimōsa no kuni go-
fushinba ichiran*, 'Canal
Construction at a Glance in
the Shimōsa Province'. Artist:
Baiei, the daughter of Suzuki.
Orihon rebound from a roll,
ink and colour on paper; 1843.
Ex-Siebold collection.
[16084.e.10]

34
Stencil-dyeing *obi* (sashes for *kimono*). From *Yamato shinō ezukushi*. 'Complete Picture book of the Samurai and the Farmer'. Artist: Hishikawa Moronobu. One volume, partly hand-coloured (Edo, 1684). Despite the title, this book does embrace the occupations of all the four classes of society.
[Or.65.a.3]

同 打 と 園 書 か 画

同 過 錆 くとうくとうる

窯 かま

同 素 燒 そやき

35
Pottery-making in Arita, the
home of Imari wares. From
Nihon sankai meisan zue,
'Noted Products from Land
and Sea of Japan in Pictures'.
Artist: Shitomi Kangetsu.
Five volumes (Osaka, 1799). A
Meiji wood-block recut for a
facsimile reproduction in
orihon format (i.e. without the
central division) is shown on
the inside covers. However,
the right-hand and the left-
hand sides of this picture in
the original *fukurotoji* edition
as illustrated here were
printed from two separate
blocks (*see* Introduction).
[16035.c.6]

36 *(Overleaf)*:
Leisure outings at Asukayama. From *Tōto shōkei ichiran*, 'Fine Views of the
Estern Capital at a Glance'. One of the three poetic topographical works by
Hokusai depicting the famous sights of Edo, to which the accompanying *kyōka*
poems are quite subsidiary. Three volumes, colour-printed (Edo, 1800).
Asukayama was a beauty spot especially set aside by the Shogunate for cherry-
blossom viewings by the people of Edo. The stone monument commemorating its
origin still stands today.
[16099.c.58]

巴曲亭桃李書

元亨山
日ゝうし
もゝ
花の雪
ひてうし
よろうん碑の
文字

雀暐永喜

求つと
ともうめ
さくろろ花
阿のうり
隣一目なり
くむうミん

40

飛鳥山

佐羽亭幾之

41

37
Edo dwellers bemused by the strange sight of Dutchmen in their lodgings, from *Azuma asobi*, the
'Pleasures of the East', another topographical *kyōka-bon* illustrated by Hokusai. One volume
(Edo, 1799). [16099.c.82]

38

An American naval officer and marine as seen through Japanese eyes. From *Gaiban yōbō zue*, 'Pictures of the Appearance of Foreign Barbarians', illustrated by Tagawa Shundō. Two volumes, colour-printed (Edo, 1854). One of the many books produced immediately after the visit of Commodore Perry to inform the Japanese about the people of the West.

[16113.d.47]

39

The procession of the Korean envoy (top) and an equestrian entertainment in their honour. One of 100 large oblong plates from *Karaku saiken-zu*, 'Detailed Views of the Flowering Capital in Pictures'. Attributed to Ōmori Yoshikiyo. Fifteen *maki* in 12 *orihon* albums; 1705 (preface 1704; colophon 1703), Kyoto.

[Or.65.c.4]

Nature and landscapes

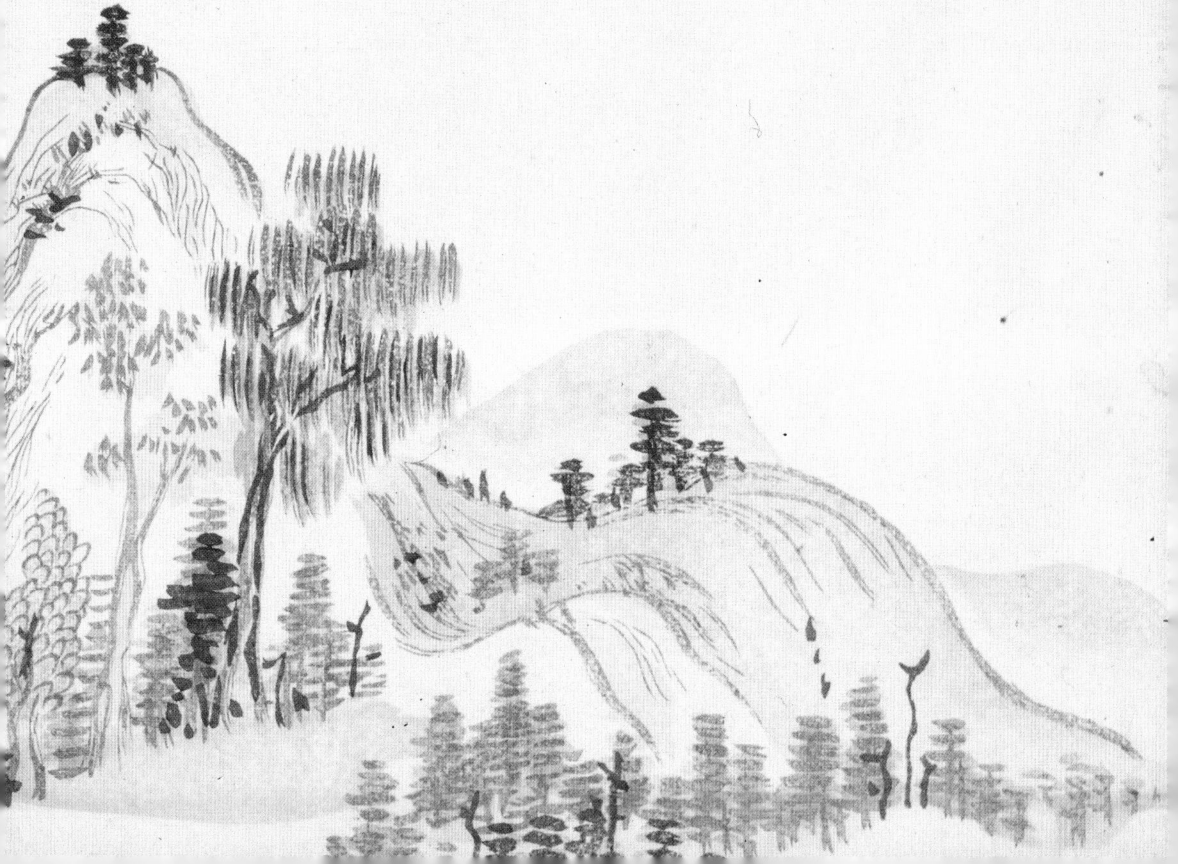

Whereas the West has traditionally placed man above nature, the Japanese have felt part of it. Living on a long archipelago with volcanoes, earthquakes and sharp climatic contrasts, they have learned to adapt to nature with sensibility. Zen teaches that, within Nature's embrace, man must first discover himself. Shintoism, on the other hand, believes that all things have spirit and deserve respect. Almost every *waka* and *haiku* poem alludes to the changing seasons, and in many arts and crafts – flower arrangement, the tea ceremony, cuisine, garden layout and so on – nature is recreated in miniature. It is not surprising, therefore, that *kachō-e* (pictures of flowers and birds) and *sansui-ga* (pictures of mountain and water landscapes) are dominant genres in paintings as well as in book illustrations.

All schools of art portrayed the natural world. Flowers, birds, insects, fishes and animals were common themes for the Kanō and Shijō, while landscapes were a special preserve of the *Nanga*. Even *Ukiyo-e* artists produced outstanding prints of *kachō* and landscape subjects, despite their preoccupation with contemporary urban lives. Especially fine examples of the latter are Utamaro's renowned 'Insects Book' (*Ehon mushi erami*) and 'Shell Book' (*Shioi no tsuto*); and Hokusai's views of Edo as backdrops for human pleasure (36; 67; 68). As a rule, the mode of these *Ukiyo-e* portrayals was representational realism, the diametric opposite of the contemplative abstraction of the *Nanga* and the spontaneous naturalism of the Shijō. The latter is exemplified by Mori Tetsuzan's dramatic close-up of a pair of mallards which appears in one of the loveliest and rarest Shijō albums produced in Kyoto, the *Ranpō-jō* (50).

The essence of *Nanga* landscape is well conveyed by two prints (40; 75) from *Taigadō gafu*, the 'Drawing Book of Taigadō', an album regarded as a sublime expression of *Nanga* printed art. Published in 1803, long after the death of Ike Taiga (1723–75), it consists of the master's drawings of trees, landscapes and rocks as well as figure studies adapted by his follower, Sō Geppō (1760–1839). Taiga's instinct for evocative settings, by means of asymmetrical placement and abstract patterns as well as subtle colours, brought the Chinese landscapes within the comprehension of his countrymen. Mixed subjects of fruit, bamboo, flower, insect, bird, animal, as well as landscape – traditional favourites for Chinese-style instructional manuals – were likewise 'Japanised' by numerous *Nanga* masters, including the eclectic Tani Bunchō (1763–1840) (45) and Tatebe Ryōtai (1719–94) (48). By contrast, Okada Baikan (1784–1844), chose to devote his entire album to the praise of the beauty of plum-blossom (47), also in a thoroughly graphic and unmistakably Japanese style.

Meanwhile, Itō Jakuchū (1716–1800), best known for his realistic paintings of barnyard fowl, was credited with first exploiting the

40 *(Pages 44–5)*:
A sublime mountain landscape in *Nanga* style by Ike no Taiga (slightly enlarged). From *Taigadō gafu*, the 'Taigadō's Drawing Book', adapted by his pupil Sō Geppō in printed medium. *Orihon* album, lightly colour-printed (Kyoto, 1804). [Or.64.a.18]

41
Tree pony, with calligraphic Chinese poem. From *Soken sekisatsu*, 'Dazzling Simplicity in Stone Prints'. Designed by Itō Jakuchū in style of a stone-rubbing. *Orihon* album, white-on-black *ishizuri* prints; a slightly later recut edition of the 1768 original, Kyoto. [Or.64.a.11]

42
Water plantain. From *Soken gafu: sōka no bu*, 'Soken's Drawing Book: Plant Section', by Yamaguchi Soken. Three volumes, gradated *sumi* printing (Kyoto, 1806). [16111.c.10]

千瓣開幽睦春風
滑玉雲由来宰相
名卉向山中著

43

Trumpet flower. From *Ka'i*, the 'Vocabulary of Flowers', compiled and illustrated by Shimada Mitsufusa and Ono Ransan. Eight volumes, European style hand-colouring added; 1750 (vols I–IV: grass section) and 1765 (vols IV–VIII: tree section), Kyoto. Ex-Siebold collection. [16033.e.6]

44

Irises and water plantains. From *Ehon noyamagusa*, 'Picture-book of Wild Flowers', by Tachibana Yasukuni, Kanō School. Five volumes, colour-printed (Osaka, 1883). This botanical compendium was first published in black and white in 1755. One hundred and twenty-eight years later, the original blocks were partially reused as key blocks together with the newly cut colour blocks which were designed by Hasegawa Sadanobu, an *Ukiyo-e* artist. An interesting and rare hybrid edition. [16033.a.15]

45
Lily. from *Shazanrō ehon*,
'Drawing book of
Shazanrō', nature studies
by Tani Bunchō. One
volume, *sumizuri* and
lightly colour-printed
(Edo, Kyoto and Osaka,
1816). Shazanrō was one of
Bunchō's art names. A
poet and an eclectic painter
and prolific book
illustrator, he was also
credited with introducing
Nanga style to Edo.
[16115.d.13]

unusual technique known as *ishizuri* ('stone printing') in his two
astonishingly beautiful albums. *Soken sekisatsu*, 'Stone Prints of Dazzling Simplicity' (41) is one of them and contains 36 double-page open-
ings, each with a floral design on the left, accompanied by a Chinese
poem in stylish calligraphy on the right-hand page. These were printed
from wood-blocks but in imitation of Chinese stone-rubbing, with the
striking effect of white reserve on a black background, hence the name.

Kachō-e picture books were a particularly fertile genre in which to
experiment with various techniques to induce gradations in printed
texture. Among them were what Jack Hillier calls the 'trituration' and
'lowering' ploys. *Soken gafu: sōka no bu*, 'Soken's Drawing Book: Plant
Section' is a sophisticated example of the former. His image of large
leaves for instance, gained added power from the block-cutter attack-
ing his surface to produce a rough, mezzotint-like effect (42). It is in the
books of nature and landscapes that we see, too, the earliest successful
attempts at colour printing. Both the 1746 first edition of the 'Living
Garden of Ming Painting' (46) by Ōoka Shunboku (1680–1763) and

Ryūsui's 'Boon of the Sea' of 1762 (**51**), already mentioned in connection with *haiku* books, antedated the more well-known 'brocade' printing of Harunobu's Yoshiwara beauties of 1770 (*see* front cover).

All the floral examples so far discussed have no other purpose than visual enjoyment. But there were more strictly botanical studies by artists of other schools, notably the Kanō. However, the five-volume 'Wild Flowers' by Tachibana Yasukuni (1717–92), first published in 1755, had no pretension to botanical accuracy, the Kanō artist just being concerned with the decorative aspect of his composition (**44**). A similarly high standard of composition can be claimed for *Ka'i*, a 'Vocabulary of Plants' (**43**) and for the *Sōmoku kihin kagami* (*see* title page). The latter amounts to a catalogue of rare specimens of plants and trees published by a plant-seller, Kinta, who commissioned artists of note for their illustrations. Both books were tastefully hand-coloured which enlivened the already effective use of the black and white medium.

46
Banana plant, rock and grass. From *Minchō seidō gaen*, 'The Living Garden of Ming Painting', a manual for floral paintings by Ōoka Shunboku after Ming masters. Three volumes, colour-printed largely from recut blocks (*c*.1813, Kyoto). The rare 1746 original edition was produced by mixed methods of stencil and colour blocks.
[Or.65.a.24]

47
A forest of plum-blossoms. From *Baika-jō*, 'Picture-album of Plum Blossom'. A *haiku* book illustrated by Okada Baikan, a poet and *Nanga* artist. One volume, gradated *sumi* printing (Kyoto, 1808). Pine-tree, bamboo and the plum-blossom were the literati's best loved triad. Baikan's obsession with this flower was reflected by his other pen-names: Baikan Bokusha, the 'Shepherd among the plum-blossom'; and Baikaen, 'Garden of plum-blossom'.
[16116.d.1]

猫睨咬鳥

48
A cat pounces at its prey.
From *Kanyōsai gafu*,
'Drawing Book of Kanyōsai'.
Nature studies by Tatebe
Ryōtai, *haiku* poet, scholar and
Nanga artist. Five volumes
(Edo, 1762).
[16111.c.15]

49
Kumataka, a type of falcon,
catching a monkey. From
Nigri kobushi, 'The Clenched
Fist'. A manual of falconry,
based on an anonymous Kanō
work published in 1687. One
volume; *c.*1750, n.p.
[16035.b.7]

青とらいひ征鳥といひ

ス晨風といふとてうて代々

よりていへる名おほくて遣

とりてはそれなりとも遣

ふくい牧名牧種

のたうばりてもに明らててに

四十八種よりいひか

セら今和漢あわ鷙の

たちれも名ぐことく

くにおかうとうた

の

〇鷹の諸名

<table>
<tr><td>大鷹</td><td>小鷹</td><td>鷂</td></tr>
<tr><td>角鷹</td><td>鷲</td><td>鵰</td></tr>
<tr><td>隼</td><td>鴟</td><td>鳶</td></tr>
<tr><td>雄鷹</td><td>鵲</td><td>鵰</td></tr>
<tr><td>鵠</td><td>鷂</td><td>鵠</td></tr>
<tr><td>山鷂</td><td>鶻</td><td>鵜</td></tr>
</table>

角鷹（くまたか）

53

50
A dramatic close-up of
mallards in a stream, with a
diminutive peasant crossing a
plank bridge in the far left
corner. From *Ranpō-jō*, the
'Album of the Fabulous Bird',
a *haiku*, anthology, illustrated
by Soken, Tetsuzan
(reproduced here), Hōen,
Rankō and Nangaku. One
volume, colour-printed
(Kyoto, 1806).
[Or.64.a.10]

51

Itoyori-dai, cockles, clams, and crabs, with calligraphic *haiku*. From *Umi no sachi*, the 'Boon of the Seas'. A *haiku* anthology on fish and shellfish, illustrated by Katsuma Ryūsui. Two volumes; colour-printed with mica (to give the sheen of the fish), (Edo, 1762). Comparatively little is known of this amateur painter, except for his two other exceptionally beautiful books of nature studies. The subtle colour-printing anticipated the advent of Harunobu's brilliant 'brocade prints' of 1770. [16115.d.17]

Women's world

52
Ladies playing a *koto*, a *biwa*
and a zither, with a singer,
while a teacher looks on. From
Tsubo no ishibumi, 'The Stone
Inscription of Tsubo', a book
of ethical and practical
instructions for women. Artist:
Ishikawa Ryūsen, *Ukiyo-e*
school. Thirteen volumes
(Edo, 1698).
[16124.d.30]

Edo Japan was a world of men obsessed with women. The delicate black-and-white books produced in Kamigata (the Kyoto–Osaka region) by such prolific early illustrators as Nishikawa Sukenobu (1671–1751), depict not just the courtesans but also women of all vocations and classes, from empress, to priestess, to farmer's wife (**54**). However, the portrayals of beautiful and finely dressed women of the pleasure quarters remained the central theme of multi-colour prints, books and albums of the Edo-based *Ukiyo-e* from the 1770s onwards. The masterpieces of Yoshiwara beauties by Suzuki Harunobu, Torii Kiyonaga (1752–1815), Kubo Shunman (1757–1820), Hosoi Eishi (1756–1829) (**63**) and, ultimately, by Utamaro (**61; 66**), became so well known in the West as to seem to stereotype all Japanese women. How far they themselves pursued the courtesan ideal is a good cultural and psychological question. Certainly, the *demi-monde* of the licensed quarters made a big impact on the rest of womenfolk, for the courtesan was no mere prostitute but an arbiter of taste in music, poetry, calligraphy and wit, as well as fashion. Her elegant allure, exotically portrayed, made her the idol of the entire nation.

Almost from the beginning of commercial publishing in the mid-17th century, illustrated textbooks containing knowledge every woman should acquire flourished alongside guides to the pleasure quarters

53
Mother supervising her
daughters in choosing a new
uchikake (a long outer
garment), with the latest
fashion book beside her. From
Ehon Edo murasaki, 'Picture-
book of the Violet of Edo'. A
useful book for women,
compiled by Tokusōshi of
Naniwa, and illustrated by the
Ukiyo-e artist, Ishikawa
Toyonobu (1711–85). Three
volumes (Kyoto, Osaka and
Edo, 1765). Violet was the
colour for nobility, thus
symbolising the excellence of
womanly virtues.
[Or.65.c.41]

published solely for men. The former appear as *ōraimono* (literally, 'go
and come' thing, meaning correspondence) and *kyōkun* (didactics),
both intended to teach women behaviour and etiquette in a moralistic
fashion. *Tsubo no islibumi* by Ishikawa Ryūsen (*fl.c.*1687–1713) (**52**)
and Hanbei's *Joyō kinmō zuī* (**56**) are typical of these multi-volume
encyclopedias on womanly virtues and accomplishments, from playing
the *koto* to folding one's *kimono* in the right order. Criticism of bad
women equally appears. Despite the official Confucian ethic which
expected women to be submissive, humble, frugal and hard-working,
women of the Edo period did benefit much, materially as well as
intellectually, from lively social and economic change. The ever inno-
vative textile and craft industries yielded beautiful objects for the
fashion-conscious women of the new middle class, hence the oppor-
tunity for *Ukiyo-e* and other designers to express their decorative flair
in numerous pattern books. Indeed, certain artistic geniuses, such as
Ogata Kōrin (1658–1716), devoted a lifetime to the designing of
kimono fabrics, combs and other feminine accessories (**56; 57; 58**).

As education spread, not least through the village schools (*terakoya*)
(**59**), Japanese women achieved a level of literacy high for pre-modern
society. It was estimated that, by the end of the Edo period, 15 per cent

ゑちよく
芳巴石
山ぬるゝ

57 *(Right)*:
Exquisite designs of combs. From *Makie taizen*, 'A Complete Book of Lacquer Designs', illustrated by Ōoka Shunsen, Kanō school. Five volumes (Osaka, 1759). This book contains a mine of information on Japanese designs, many of which are by Kōrin, the master of the decorative Rinpa school.
[16110.e.20]

58
Kimono patterns in zodiac symbols (right) and in *ashibune* (boat among the reeds), a classical design with literary associations. From *Shinsen o-hiinagata*, a 'New Selection of Respected Patterns'. Illustrator anonymous; preface by Asai Ryōi, a pioneer of popular fiction. Two volumes (Kyoto, 1667). Another important work also in the history of colour printing in that rudimentary single-colour printing was applied with pale blue, olive green (e.g. for zodiac pattern), and russet red.
[Or.74.cc.8]

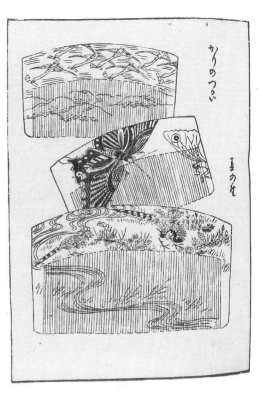

59
Segregated class-rooms for boys and girls at a village school. From *Ehon jogei sōshi*, 'Picture-book of Female Talents'. Written by an authoress Hayashi Ranjo, and illustrated by Nishikawa Sukenobu. Three volumes (Osaka, 1742). [Or.65.a.17]

四德とい
仁義
孔智と
ひろめて
わづかな
ゆくも
積てらる
知るべし

60

Girls learning the 'four virtues' through books written in simple *kana*. From *Jidō kyōkun iroha uta*, 'The Paragon of *Iroha* Alphabets for Children', illustrated by Shimokōbe Shūsui. Three volumes (Kyoto, 1775). [Or.64.c.23/3]

The floating world

The word *ukiyo* originally meant the 'fleeting world' – this transient, sad life as preached by Buddhism. By 1650, with Japan fast becoming something of a consumer society, it had acquired a new meaning, the 'floating world': a world of people drifting on a sea of pleasure. The main foci of the pleasures were the Kabuki theatre and the licensed quarters in the bustling cities of Edo and Osaka – and, to a lesser extent, Kyoto and Nagoya. The former was immensely popular with both sexes, young and old, whilst the latter had sprung up largely in response to the needs of two groups of people: the idle young *samurai* and the *nouveaux riches* merchants' sons. These establishments, known euphemistically as 'Green Houses' (*seirō*), were to become centres of elegant amusement as well as earthier pleasures. The great houses (the grandest being the Yoshiwara, on the north-east side of Edo) were presided over by expensive courtesans who were, as remarked earlier, renowned for their charm, wit, and artistic skills as well as for their physical beauty. They were the subjects of innumerable *Ukiyo-e* paintings and prints, as well as books and albums.

Courtesan critiques – a kind of pictorial *Who's who* – with commentary on looks, behaviour and price were among the earliest types of printed *Ukiyo-e*. Indeed, the demand for them greatly stimulated a boom in colour printing after that technique had been perfected in Edo around 1765. Henceforward, a long list of masterpieces depicting the Yoshiwara, in rich and fascinating detail, included the oft-quoted Harunobu's *Ehon seirō bijin awase*; the famous *Sierō bijin awase sugata kagami*, 'Mirror of Beautiful Women of the Green Houses', 1776, a collaborative work by Katsukawa Shunshō (1726–92) and Kitao Shigemasa (1739–1820); Masanobu's *Yoshiwara keisei shin bijin awase jihitsu kagami*, 1784; and Utamaro's *Seirō ehon nenjū gyōji* (**61**). The text of the last named was by Jippensha Ikku, a great humorist and leading man of letters in Edo. He and Utamaro are known to have frequently ventured at night into the Yoshiwara district; their combined knowledge of its affairs all the year round yielded this, one of the most famous books on the life of the pleasure quarters (*see also* 1).

Some extraordinarily handsome albums combining *kyōka* poetry with pictures of courtesans by *Ukiyo-e* artists were published from the 1770s onwards. Eishi's contribution in *Yanagi no ito* (**63**) is an especially endearing image: a grand courtesan parading in all her finery through the thoroughfare of Yoshiwara in the new year, flanked by her attendants. Such prints are veritable fashion-plates.

If the great courtesans were the heroines of the floating world, the Kabuki actors were its heroes. The Kabuki has always been an actor-centred theatre; its devotees coming not so much to see plots unfold as to admire their favourite stars in familiar roles, often handed down within a family from one generation to the next. The fans' desire to

65

64
The gallery of Kabuki
theatre, by Utamaro.
Frontispiece to *(Niago ehon)*
yakusha gakuya-tsū,
'Likeness Portraits of Actors
Pictured in Their Dressing
Rooms'. Biographies of the 36
actors of the day by Shikitei
Sanba, with portraits by
Toyokuni and Kunimasa. One
volume, colour-printed (Edo,
1799). Sanba, a writer of light
fiction, was also an
acknowledged authority of
Kabuki plays and players.
The laid-back, pipe-smoking
theatre-goer pictured in the
gallery could well be Sanba
himself.
[16104.a.40]

follow them everywhere stimulated 'critiques of actors' which presented them both on and off stage. Thus, Shunshō's *Yakusha natsu no
Fuji*, 'Actors like Fuji in Summer', 1780, showed actors engaging in all
kinds of non-theatrical pursuits and recreation. Its resounding success
was reflected in a succession of books in a similar vein designed by
Toyokuni and his pupil Kunisada (1786–1864) **(62; 64; 65)**. Theatrical
picture books such as these had an advantage over single-sheet actor
prints (more familiar in the West) in that a fan could follow his hero's
comings and goings page-by-page, just like a colour television.

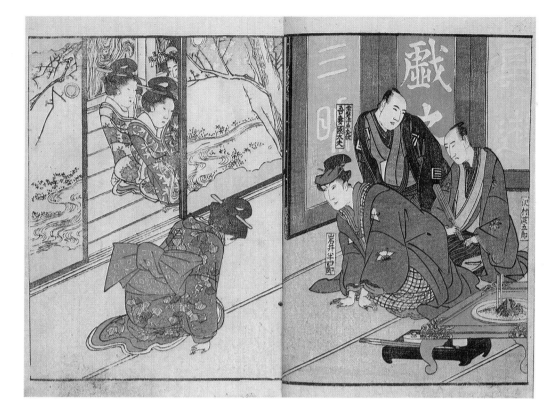

65

Iwai Hanshirō, a famous
female impersonator of the
Kabuki, and his companions
paying a New Year visit to the
household of a rich patron.
From *Yakusha sangai-kyō*,
'Amusements of Actors on the
Third Floor', written by
Shikitei Sanba and illustrated
by Toyokuni. Two volumes,
colour-printed (Edo, 1801).
Another theatrical book
produced to satisfy the intense
public craving for intimate
views of the lives of the actors
off-stage and back-stage. The
'third floor' housed the actors'
dressing rooms.
[16104.a.37]

66 *(Pages 70–71):*

Courtesans feeding a caged
bird on a verandah, with a
screen decorated with a view
of Fuji in the background. A
maid is holding up a pestle, a
suggestive object which
always provoked ribald
laughter. From *Otoko-dōka*,
'Stamping Song of Men'. A
kyōka anthology on the New
Year, with prints by Utamaro
(illustrated), Shigemasa, Eishi,
Hokusai, Tōrin and Ekiji. De
luxe *orihon* album, colour-
printed (Edo, 1797).
[16099.c.84]

67

Mother and child weaving in the countryside with Mt Fuji in the background. From *Shunkyō-jō*, 'Album of Spring Amusement'. A *kyōka* anthology on the New Year, with prints by Shiransai, Hokusai (illustrated), and Shigemasa. One volume, colour-printed; no date given, *c.* 1798, no place of publication, but probably Edo. A very rare book which also contains one of Hakusai's neglected masterpieces, showing soft colours and the imaginative use of space. [16099.c.87]

68

Courtesans using a telescope to get a close view of the racecourse at Takada, on the outskirts of Edo. From *Ehon kyōka yama mata yama*, 'Picture-book of *Kyōka: Mountains upon Mountains*'. A *kyōka* anthology illustrated by Hokusai, who here used landscapes as backdrops for his figure studies. Three volumes, colour-printed (Edo, 1804). [16099.c.59]

The golden age of Japanese book illustration can be said to span from 1780 to 1830, the decades in which colour printing and art-book publishing reached their peak. The vogue for *kyōka* 'crazy verses' among the leisured *chōnin* of Edo brought forth the most beautiful picture books (*ehon*), combining anthologies of *kyōka* with illustrations by leading *Ukiyo-e* artists. Meanwhile, in Kyoto, the centre of the 'classical' school of *Nanga* and Shijō, exquisite *haiku* books as well as *gafu* albums, with prints of the brushwork of past and living masters, flourished as never before. Some of the finest *kyōka-bon* were the result of the dedication of one publisher, Tsutaya Jūsaburō (1750–97). A leading figure in the literary and artistic circles of the Yoshiwara pleasure quarters, he had a workshop in their vicinity where he gathered round him some of the most talented writers, artists, block-cutters and printers of the day. It was virtually under his roof, in 1783–97, that Utamaro designed his rightly celebrated 'Insect Book' and the 'Shell Book'; and his trilogy on the autumn moon (*Kyōgetsubō*), winter snow (*Ginsekai*) and spring blossoms (*Fugenzō*), all of which can be seen in the British Museum. The trilogy belongs to the genre of *kyōka* anthology published in celebration of the New Year or other annual festivals. This genre was established by the success of his *Kyōka waka ebisu* (1789) (**73**), one of the earliest *kyōka-bon* he did for Tsutaya.

Utamaro apart, Tsutaya enjoyed the friendship and services of many leading *Ukiyo-e* artists, including Eishi, Hokusai, Shunman, Shigemasa, and Tsutsumi Tōrin (*c.* 1743–1820). *Kyōka* books by Hokusai, illustrating the landscapes and customs of Edo such as *Tōto shōkei ichiran*, 1800 (**36**), and *Ehon kyōka yama mata yama*, 1804 (**68**) – were published under Tsutaya's imprint, albeit posthumously. Here one sees an early manifestation of Hokusai's prowess in landscape drawing expressed so daringly 20 years later in his 'Thirty-Six Views of Mount Fuji'.

Another mode of publication at which Tsutaya excelled was collaborative albums by several artists. These joint works were produced with infinite care on large-size sheets of quality paper. The illustrations, usually no more than five or six per book, were elaborately colour-printed on a double spread. The accompanying poems were written in the finest calligraphy in perfect harmony with the illustrations. It was in these de luxe albums that some of the best-known and admired *Ukiyo-e* illustrations were executed. Utamaro's memorable print of 'Courtesans feeding a caged bird' in *Otoko dōka* (**66**); Eishi's 'Courtesan parading in the new year' in *Yanagi no ito* (*see page 64*), (**63**); Tōrin's 'Warrior Asahina reclining' in *Momo saezuri* (*see back cover*); and Hokusai's tender 'Mother and child weaving in the countryside' in the rare *Shunkyō-jō* (**67**) are just a few examples. Tsutaya's sumptuous *kyōka-bon* were the book equivalent of *surimono*, the exquisitely decorated sheet prints commissioned for distribution as gifts for special occasions, such as the New Year, within exclusive clubs.

In Kyoto from around 1800, a burgeoning cultural sophistication, and especially a renewed appreciation of the works of old masters, led to a rush for *gafu*. By a happy chance, wood-block printing had by then evolved into a truly definitive means of reproducing faithfully the flowing brush strokes that exemplified *Nanga* and Shijō virtuosity. One notable result was the revival of Rinpa – the decorative style of painting pioneered by Ogata Kōrin. In his *Kōrin gafu* published in 1802, a Rinpa painter and *haiku* poet, Nakamura Hōchū (*fl.c.*1790–1820) recaptured the exceptional quality of the originals by highlighting Kōrin's dramatic simplifications **(69)**. Thereafter, a succession of works by such seminal figures as Kanō Tan'yū (1602–74), Shōkadō (1584–1639), Taigadō and Ōkyo were published for the first time. The *Taigadō gafu* (*see* page 46), **(40)** and **(75)**, is a striking reinterpretation of the original.

Side-by-side with their 'facsimiles' of past masters, contemporary artists in Kyoto, Osaka and Nagoya turned to *gafu* to propagate their styles. Tatebe Ryōtai's *Kanyōsai gafu* **(48)**, Tani Bunchō's *Shazanrō*

69
Nobleman with attendant crossing a bridge. From *Kōrin gafu*, 'A Book of Paintings by Kōrin', adapted for the printed medium by Nakamura Hōchū. Two *orihon* albums, colour-printed (Edo, 1802). The first of the major books which led the revival of the decorative Rinpa style. A triumphant transformation of Kōrin's water colours by means of wood-blocks.
[British Museum: OA 489]

70
Street singers soliciting alms, while passers-by turn a deaf ear. From *Kishi enpu*, 'Mr Aoi's Chronicle of Charm'. A *haiku* anthology on the life of the Shinmachi pleasure quarters, illustrated by Saitō Shūho of the Shijō school. Three volumes, colour-printed (Osaka, 1803). [British Museum OA 515A].

ehon (45); Bōsai's visionary *Kyōchū-zan*, 'Mountains of the Heart'; and Ki Chikudō's *Chikudō gafu* (71) were among the finest *Nanga* examples. The lyrical beauty of the *bunjin* landscapes in the last, enhanced by the crayon-like pigments, was a tribute to the skill of both block-cutter and printer.

However, it was Shijō artists that led to the Kyoto-Osaka region becoming once again an art publishing centre to rival Edo. Yamaguchi Soken's marvellously impromptu studies of all types of Japanese people in *Yamato jinbutsu gafu* (26) of 1800 ushered in a new era of graphic art. The exuberant prints on a diversity of subjects by Bunpō, Kihō, Suiseki, Chinnen, Nantei, Koshū and a whole tribe of Shijō talents have been well celebrated by Jack Hillier in his *The Uninhibited Brush*. For example, Saitō Shūho's hilarious masterpiece, the *Kishi enpu* (70), satirises candidly the none-too-elegant life of the Shinmachi brothel district in Osaka, thus challenging the idealised 'floating world' as seductively portrayed by the *Ukiyo-e* printmakers of Edo.

The role of *haiku* in illustrated books by *Nanga* and Shijō artists has already been considered (*see* pages 20 to 29). But *Sho-meika shoga-fu* (72) brings us to 'communal' albums once again. They are books of great beauty and interest comparable to Tsutaya's de luxe *kyōka-bon*. To the *Sho-meika* album, Uchida Gentai(1749–1822) persuaded a number of literati friends to contribute their drawings and calligraphy in celebration of his 70th and 71st birthdays. It is in *gassaku* 'joint work' such as this that rare gems by little-known artists of great virtuosity can be discovered. For example, the 1803 *Tokai-jō* (74), the 'Album of the Capital', concealed one print by the illusive Saito Shūho of *Kishi enpu* fame. Because he used a different name, Ichiami, for this print, it has not, up to now, been recognised as his work by historians. But further examination of the seal affixed reveals that it reads 'Ichiami Sōkyū' – Sōkyū being Shūho's other art name. This spirited *haiku* anthology contains ten other prints by such *Shijō* masters as Bunpō, Nantei and Baitei, as well as by some artists whose identities have yet to be unravelled. It is also exceedingly rare, with only two copies known to be extant. The British Library's copy is in pristine condition with the strong, clear colours unfaded. The prints depicting various comic *Nō*

71
A lake landscape with typical *bunjin* figures and the accompanying Chinese poem. From *Chikudō gafu*, 'Drawing Book of Chikudō'. Two albums, colour-printed (Kyoto, 1800 and 1815 respectively). One of the finest illustrated books produced by the *Nanga* school.
[16116.b.25]

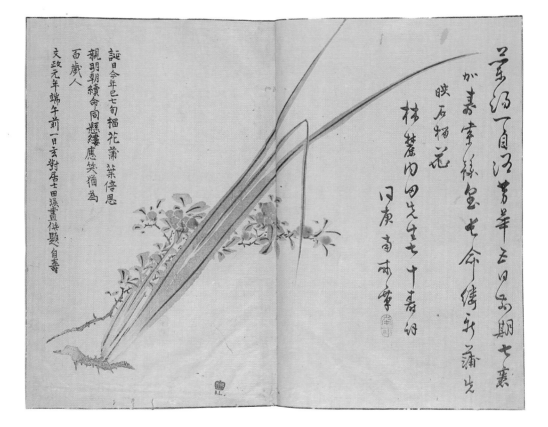

誕日今年巳七旬榴花蒲葉倍思
親朋朝續命同懸縷應笑猶為
百歲人
文政元年端午前一日玄對居士田喓畫係題
自壽

72
Pomegrante and iris, by Uchida Gentai, with a calligraphic poem by himself and a
eulogy by Nanpo (right). From *Sho-meika shoga-fu*, 'An album of Calligraphy and
Paintings by Various Masters'. Contributed by Bunchō, Bōsai, Nankō, Bunpō
and others in celebration of Gentai's birthdays. De luxe album, partly colour-
printed (no place of publication but probably Edo, 1819). A good example of a
private publication of joint works in which artists' original seals were affixed. A
comparison of the three known copies in Western collections reveals discrepancies
in the number of pictures, the order in which they were presented and clear
variations in certain of the artists' seals.
[Or.81.c.25]

scenes are so fresh and vigorous as to be positively avant-garde. *Tokai-
jō* epitomises the new Shijō style which combined compelling design
with sharp cutting, printing and intricate colours to effect some of the
most beautiful book illustrations ever produced in any country.

73

A performing monkey clad in
female fashion entertains the
household of a *daimyō* in the
New Year. Watching in
amusement are the daughter
and her attendant sitting
behind the transparent screen.
From *Ehon waka ebisu*,
'Picture-book of Young
Ebisu'. A *kyōka* anthology on
the theme of early spring,
illustrated by Utamaro. De
luxe *orihon* album, colour-
printed with gauffrage, gold
and silver leaf (Edo, 1789).
The silhouettes behind the
screen, the inclusion of a
picture within a picture in the
form of a *tsuitate* stand, and
the deliberate Tosa-style cloud
formations all make this one of
the most memorable of
Utamaro's book-prints.
[16099.c.76]

74 (*Opposite above*):
Ohara girls dancing beside their
bundles of brushwood and exciting
the interests of two men, by nantei.

(*Opposite below*):
A man being caught while stealing
flowers for his lover, by Ichiami
Sōkyū, alias Saitō Shūho of *Kishi
enpu* fame (**70**). All the characters in
both pictures wear masks as they
would appear in a *kyōgen* farce.
From *Tokai-jō*, 'The Album of the
Capital'. A *haiku* anthology, with 11
prints by several Sijō artists. De
luxe *orihon* album; colour-printed
(Kyoto, 1803).
[16099.f.32]

Suggestions for further reading

Brown, Louise Norton, *Block Printing and Book Illustrations in Japan* (Routledge, London, 1924; Minkoff Reprint, Geneva, 1973).

Cahill, James, *Scholar Painters of Japan* (Asia House Library, New York, 1972).

Chibbett, David, *The History of Japanese Printing and Book Illustration* (Kodansha International, Tokyo, 1977).

Forrer, Matthi, *Eirakuya Tōshirō, Publisher at Nagoya* (J.C. Gieben, Publisher, Amsterdam, 1985).

Hibbett, Howard, *The Floating World in Japanese Fiction* (Charles E. Tuttle Co. Tokyo, 1975; first edition, Oxford University Press, London, 1959).

Hillier, Jack, *The Uninhibited Brush: Japanese Art in the Shijo Style* (Hugh M. Moss, London, 1974).

The Art of Hokusai in Book Illustration (Sotheby's, London; University of California Press, Los Angeles, 1980).
The Art of the Japanese Book (Sotheby's, London, 1987).

Hillier, Jack and Smith, Lawrence, *Japanese Prints: 300 Years of Albums and Books* (British Museum, London, 1980).

Holloway, Owen E. *Graphic Art of Japan: The Classical School* (Transatlantic, London, 1957).

Lane, Richard, *Images from the Floating World: the Japanese Print* (Oxford University Press, Oxford, London, Melbourne, 1978).

Mitchell, C.H., *The Illustrated Books of The Nanga, Maruyama and Shijo and Other Related Schools of Japan: A Bibliography* (Dawson's Bookshop, Los Angeles, 1972).

Okuda, Hideo, *Emaki: Japanese Picture Scrolls*, translated by John Bester and Charles Pomeroy (Charles E. Tuttle, Tokyo, 1962).

Toda, Kenji, *Descriptive Catalogue of the Japanese and Chinese Illustrated Books in the Ryerson Library* (Art Institute of Chicago, Chicago, 1931).

Waterhouse, D.B., *Harunobu and His Age: The Development of Colour Printing in Japan* (British Museum, London, 1964).

75
Tree landscape. From *Taigadō gafu*
(For description *see* **40** and p. **46**)